3

fly   nudges an apple
                    jamjar.
dougal shaves a downy cheek, touches
again (in his mind) small
                    softness, mary's breast.
wild collie, blood on his jaw, stalks
                    another
                            newborn lamb.

him with the case full of maps   is buying the place

them hammering pegs in our crofts   are his servants

4.
mountain spring
                    goes
                            seaward
meeting
          other streams, takes
in its flow some
              curlew droppings
                        bones of lamb
                                and twigs

lawn trimmings, empty bottles
                    cans, used condoms, offal
sewage, logs, car-bodies, factory waste, dead salmon.
in the firth
          (again) the migrant ships

Also by aonghas macneacail

POETRY

Poetry Quintet: Gollancz, 1976: Poems in English (anthology)
imaginary wounds: Print Studio Press, 1980: Poems in English
sireadh bradain sicir/ seeking wise salmon: Balnain Books, 1983: Poems in Gaelic
(with parallel text English translations by the author, illustrations by
Simon Fraser)
an cathadh mor/ the great snowbattle: Balnain Books, 1984: Poems in Gaelic
(with parallel text English translations by the author, illustrations by
Simon Fraser)
an seachnadh/ the avoiding: Lines Review Editions 1986: Poems in Gaelic
(with parallel text English translations by the author)
rock and water: Polygon, 1990: Poems in English
oideachadh ceart/ a proper schooling: Polygon, 1996: Poems in Gaelic (with paral-
lel text English translations by the author)
Leabhar Mor na Gaidhlig/ The Great Book of Gaelic: Canongate, 2002: Consult-
ing Editor
laoidh an donais oig/ hymn to a young demon: Polygon, 2007, poems in Gaelic
(with parallel text translations in English by the author)
*laughing at the clock/ déanamh gáire ris a' chloc: new & selected poems/dáin úra
agus thaghta*: Polygon, 2012 poems in Gaelic (with parallel text translations
in English by the author)
ayont the dyke: a pamphlet of thirty poems in Scots, Kettilonia, 2012

PROSE

A Writers' Ceilidh: Balnain Books, 1991: (Ed) Anthology of Highland
Writing
Sgathach, the Warrior Queen: Balnain Books, 1993: retelling in English of
Gaelic folk tale (illustrated by Simon Fraser)
Scotland: A Linguistic Double Helix: European Bureau for Lesser Used
Languages, 1995: an introduction to Scotland's cultural heritage;
co-authored with Iseabail MacLeod (pamphlet)

aonghas macneacail

beyond

edited by colin bramwell

with gerda stevenson

Shearsman Books

First published in the United Kingdom in 2023 by
Shearsman Books Ltd
PO Box 4239
Swindon
SN3 9FN

Shearsman Books Ltd Registered Office
30–31 St. James Place, Mangotsfield, Bristol BS16 9JB
(this address not for correspondence)

www.shearsman.com

ISBN 978-1-84861-905-0

ACKNOWLEDGEMENTS

Thanks to the editors and publishers of the following magazines and
publications where some of these poems have previously appeared: *The Scottish
Review of Books*, *Shearsman* magazine, *Best Scottish Poems 2004*, *Best of the Best
Scottish Poems 2019* (Scottish Poetry Library), *Eddie @ 90* (Scottish Poetry
Library & Mariscat Press) and *Stepping into the Avalanche: In Memory of Hugh
MacDiarmid* (Brownsbank Press, Biggar Museums Trust)

Thanks are also due to Creative Scotland, who funded the creation of this
book through the Open Project Fund: in particular we'd like to thank
Alan Bett for his wisdom and generosity.

Special thanks also to Rob MacNeacail for initiating this project and
for all his care in helping to carry it through to completion.

ALBA | CHRUTHACHAIL

contents

introduction

This book of poems is drawn from the Scottish poet Aonghas Mac-Neacail's unpublished English-language work. As Aonghas is no longer with us, it falls to me to say a few words about this collection – about the poems it contains, and about their author and his intentions for the book.

I first saw Aonghas MacNeacail in person at the Fèis Rois, a traditional music school held every summer in Ullapool. Another Angus – the Black Isle writer Angus Dunn – pointed him out to me from across a lobby crowded with parents and other teenagers. 'That's Aonghas Dubh – Black Angus,' he said, reverently. A poet's celebrity is different to the regular variety (Les Murray called it 'a non-devouring fame') but carries its own mystique, and Aonghas's physical presence certainly carried his. The long black hair and beard had by this point turned to a striking shade of white. That famous hair had likely always added a sense of gravitas to his demeanour. Five minutes in his company would quickly puncture any sense of aloofness, however. In conversation Aonghas was warm, witty and gentle. Even towards the end of his life he retained an arrestingly genial dignity. Nevertheless, he was a legendary figure. In particular, those of us from the north of Scotland felt (and feel) a proprietorial sense when his name comes up. I read his work from a young age, and he became an influential poet for me: a figure who managed to represent his own linguistically diffuse territory in a substantial way.

In the many obituaries that appeared for him in the press, Aonghas's Gaelic work was frequently quoted. This was to be expected. The poet's fame, his celebrity, was derived from his reputation as a Gaelic man of letters. Principally he was known as a bard, though in reality he was a jobbing writer: he also worked as a journalist, librettist, songwriter, broadcaster and translator. The latter may have been key to all of these professions, particularly the poetry. Many poets translate the work of other poets, but translating one's own work when writing in Gaelic is often seen as a matter of necessity – and, by contemporary Gaelic poets like Pàdraig MacAoidh and Rody Gorman, as a potentially fertile ground to write into. These poets further dislocate meaning between texts by translating themselves in a creative, sometimes unfaithful manner. Having excommunicated himself from the rigid, authoritarian Protestantism that he came to see as a blight on his home, Aonghas welcomed all sorts of faithlessness. His poetry evidences his own sense of experimentation, play and fun. He was a democrat in all respects: although he did care about his reputation, he aimed to lessen the distance between poet and audience, which is to say, between himself and others. Posthumously, the generation of poets subsequent to Aonghas have praised him for his approachability, and for a quality of unpretentiousness in his personality. I think this praise can be extended to Aonghas's poetry, too: his literary aesthetics matched his personal philosophy in this way.

Aonghas was known as a modernising influence in Gaelic poetry. He brought influences to bear from outside the UK – principally from American poets like William Carlos Williams, e.e. cummings, Charles Olson and Robert Creeley. These influences can be felt in his English-language work also. In this book, 'american sequence', an account of a trip taken to the USA, bears witness to the territory of these influences. The sequence, like all of the poems here, is written entirely in English. Even a poem like 'coyote plays with custer's ghost', which describes a cohabitation between Native Americans and Gaels, is written without using a word of Gaelic. Instead, Aonghas chooses English for the poem. It was a choice he made frequently as a writer.

> Gaelic was my first language: I was brought up in a Gaelic-speaking community where Gaelic was the language of the home. At the age of five I was enrolled in the local school, where the teacher's first job was to teach us English, which became the language of education from then on. When I opted to study Gaelic rather than French in secondary school, having chosen Gaelic, I enrolled in a class where, at the age of 12, I was confronted by a native Gaelic-speaking teacher, surrounded by native Gaelic-speaking children, where the language of education was English. The first poetry I read at school was in English – only in secondary school did I encounter the eighteenth-century Gaelic poets, and the literary tradition of Gaelic (particularly oral/sung traditions). I was aware that in global terms there was a Gaelic tradition that was presumed to be inferior, and

thus had little status: as far as the education system was concerned, contemporary Gaelic literature was dead. On the other side, we had Shakespeare, Milton, the classics. The first poem that I ever wrote was in English – I only began to write poetry in Gaelic in my mid-20s. It had only occurred to me to write poetry in Gaelic once prompted: I saw the English poetry as being my 'serious' poetry, until I became involved in the Poetry Society in London. Then I received an invitation to come to the Gaelic college in Skye as Writer-in-Residence. That, in effect, turned me from being an English-language poet who wrote occasionally in Gaelic to being predominantly a Gaelic poet for a period of years, though my printed work as a journalist remained in English. More or less every poem that I have ever written, I have translated into English, and my Gaelic collections are published in bilingual editions. Gradually – perhaps accidentally – I began to write poetry predominantly in English again in my late forties. One English-language collection, *rock & water* was published by Birlinn in 1990. I am now in my late seventies and have regularly been writing poetry in English from after this collection was published, so currently my archive contains thirty years worth of unpublished material.

That collection, *rock & water*, contained a poem called 'the divide'. This poem meant a great deal to Aonghas, and it remains an exceptional performance.

the divide

1.
Old Donald has seen New York from seaward,
spent a winter in Archangel, been broke in Valparaíso,
has drunk till dawn with shanty blacks in Capetown,
smuggled liquor here to there, loved a dancing girl in Cairo,

and has no regrets
              except
                    that his bones are grown brittle,
his muscles stiff, his eyes cloudy.

the tramp he sailed for over 30 years
went to the breakers' yard in 1948.

now he sits in his house by the shore, listening to the gulls
looking westward, reminiscing,
                          waiting.

2.
his brother John lives inland
tending his score of lean black cattle,
playing pibrochs on a chanter:
he does not hear the crows prattle.

daily he cleans and polishes his father's bagpipes,
and never lets these pipes play reels for dancers,
but dreams
          he is the last MacCrimmon
lamenting the desolation of Boreraig.

Phillip Hobsbaum had given him positive feedback on the poem. 'Go
back to The Divide, go back to your roots, write about what you know.'
rock & water was dedicated to Hobsbaum, Anne Stevenson and Sorley
MacLean ('Mentors all'). Aonghas delighted as much in his connections
to the English-writing world as to the Gaelic world; as the account
above shows, in some way those two worlds were inseparable for him.

Aonghas's 'thirty years worth of unpublished material' provides
the material for this book, though some poems in it are taken from an
earlier stage in his writing life: 'Gaudy Jane', for instance, comes from
an old notebook that also contained poems from his first pamphlet,
'imaginary wounds', the cover of which was illustrated by Alasdair Gray,
one of Aonghas's many writer/artist friends from Glasgow. Given this,
we felt it was apposite for another illustration of Aonghas by Gray to
provide the cover for this book, too.

The above interview was conducted for a Creative Scotland application made in support of this project. We had originally planned to meet monthly: I would search his archive for poems to take forward and he would write more for the book, and also read my poetry and give feedback. Our application was approved during the first round of the pandemic, which quickly put paid to any plans for meeting face-to-face. Aonghas had struggled with poor health throughout his seventies, and by the time we could meet up it was clear that he would be unable to contribute more to the project. Three decades worth of writing would be more than sufficient to see the book through. I do still feel as though the exercise was like being mentored in some ways: Aonghas was extraordinarily generous to entrust me with this work.

I have one observation on how Aonghas's writing habits changed. In earlier interviews he talked of obsessively revising poems at a young age, but towards the end it was clearer to see that (at least for Aonghas's English poetry) his method had changed to something more akin to Norman MacCaig's model of production, where the poem comes out perfectly first time or not at all – if not, write a new poem. (MacCaig famously said that it took him 'two fags' to write a poem: i.e. 'The poem, whatever it's worth, generally comes easily and quickly and pretty often with no correction at all, and once it's on the page, that's that.') At this point I should openly admit that this is not my own way of writing poetry. Ultimately, many of these poems barely needed editing in order to make the cut, however a little editing from both myself and Gerda Stevenson, Aonghas's wife and fellow poet, was required in a few instances. Gerda's knowledge of Aonghas's work is second to none: her editorial contributions to the final manuscript for this book were absolutely essential.

Aonghas certainly followed Hobsbaum's advice: there was at least a book's worth of poetry on the subject of Skye alone. However, the wide range of locations, themes and subject matters in this collection illustrates, Aonghas certainly did not confine himself to writing about his home territory. Skye, Scotland, Carlops: such territories are the locations from which the poet views the world in its entirety. This book intends to give the reader a sense of the formal and thematic breadth of this period in his writing. Though Aonghas never forgot his roots, he had a genuinely global outlook. In this collection, poems set in Skye (and Scotland) sit alongside poems set in locations all over the world;

observations on nature make way for philosophical meditations on ageing, elegies and paeans to other Scottish poets. I have always loved Aonghas's irreverence – his deeply-held belief in pacifism, his admirably open and democratic philosophy of writing and of language. I also think he is an underrated poet of seasons: although snow was clearly his most loved element, autumn is frequently represented in his later work. Most markedly in his later work, the poet returns to the subject of love, time and time again. Aonghas had a gift for writing about all forms of love – erotic, romantic, filial, parental – the love of justice and the love of the underdog – the love that existed for the Gaelic of his home, but also the love that exists between languages, the pure love of words, and of the poem as a vessel for containing any and every variety of love.

Aonghas originally intended for this book to signal his return to the literary sphere after a long convalescence. As his health declined, he was clearly comforted by the fact that this work would see the light of day: we talked together frequently about it, until he was unable to do so. He wanted this book to correct the perception of himself as a Gaelic writer, first and foremost. Gaelic was one of his three languages – Scots and English were the others. Before we started working on the book, I visited him in Carlops, in order to interview him about the project. We both agreed that a book of English-language work might have some public utility, as proof that Scottish writing is polyglot by nature. We thought that correcting the public perception of him as a Gaelic poet entirely would also be to correct perceptions of division in the language situation in Scotland more generally. Now that the process of putting this book together has come to an end, the truth of that feels clearer, to me. Aonghas's work looks forward to a future where, as he puts it in 'last night', 'my language [will] embrace / its sister tongue'. As with any bilingual poet, the point must be made: his English poetry drew from the same source as his Gaelic work. It is the intertwining of tongues which creates the tenor of the work. Aonghas's famous poem 'tha gàidhlig bheò' ('gaelic is alive') ends with the following lines: 'ach dèan dannsa dèan dannsa / `s e obair th`ann a bhith dannsa'. 'be dancing be dancing / it is work to be dancing'. Of course the dance will require a partner. English was a partner-language to Aonghas's Gaelic. Scots was another. This linguistic hybridity defines him, as much as it defines the general tenor of Scottish literature today.

The present volume intends to prove this beyond the shadow of a doubt. 'Beyond' became a preoccupation for Aonghas in his latter years: the word appears over and over again in poems written during this period in his life. I can't help but read his interest in a 'beyond' as inseparable to the goal of this book, which is also the goal of his poetry: to move beyond binary, either/or sorts of categorisations, and approach the world in a way which might lessen the perceived differences between us all, or allow us to see them in some kind of relief. I hope this comes across in this book as strongly as in Aonghas's previous work, and that this collection can also be thought of as a tribute to its author: a remarkable, playful, polylingual Scottish poet.

Colin Bramwell

foreword: aonghas macneacail and angus nicolson

In 1973 the London-based poet then known as Angus Nicolson visited his mother in his native Skye. On the way he stopped off in Glasgow to spend time with his friends Alasdair Gray and Tom Leonard. Gray captured that moment in his portrait on the cover of this book. Gray's intriguing marginalia snakes down the left side of the page, naming the date, time, place, and company. Angus Nicolson was not yet known as Aonghas MacNeacail. Much has been made in various obituaries about him 'changing his name' officially from Angus Nicolson to Aonghas MacNeacail. What many people may not realise is that his name was always Aonghas MacNeacail, though not recognised initially as such by the British state.

This is how it happened. In 1942 when his parents went to register his birth in their home village, Uig, Isle of Skye, not a word of English would have been spoken. All three adults present – parents and registrar – were native Gaelic speakers, and being of that generation, would have spoken Gaelic to one another. His parents told the registrar their son's name – Aonghas MacNeacail. All the information would have been given in Gaelic. But in a sinister case of Orwellian 'Doublethink', everything was recorded in English. Thus a language and culture are erased.

When Aonghas went to primary school in 1947 as a monoglot Gael, only English was permitted to be spoken. He vividly remembered learning English folksongs there, such as *On Ilkley Moor Baht 'at*, and *Dashing Away With a Smoothing Iron*. At high school in Portree, his native language was on offer as a single subject foreign language – a choice between French, German or Gaelic.

I will never forget my first visit to Aonghas's home in Skye, witnessing a mind-boggling three-way conversation between my future mother-in-law, Aonghas and his sister. The mother spoke Gaelic to both son and daughter, and they spoke Gaelic to her. But within the same conversation, Aonghas and his sister spoke English to one another – the language of the primary school classroom, all those decades ago, had spilled over to the playground and inevitably the homes of that younger generation, most of whom didn't become literate in their native Gaelic.

Aonghas loved languages. He had an expansive mind, which is remarkable given his upbringing within the confines of the proscriptive Free Church of Scotland, and the narrowness of the education system he was channelled through. He charted his own course, employed as a railway clerk for British Rail before studying English Literature at Glasgow University, where he co-edited GUM magazine with Tom Leonard. Working as a housing officer in the predominantly Caribbean area of Notting Hill while engaging with the Poetry Society in London broadened his horizons further.

In common with William Neill and George Campbell Hay, whose poetry he admired, he described himself as a trilingual poet, writing in Scotland's three tongues – Gaelic, Scots and English. His pamphlet of thirty Scots language poems, *ayont the dyke*, was published by Kettilonia in 2012.

His poetry was his passport, and took him far beyond these shores – to Japan, the USA, Canada, Russia, and to many countries across Europe.

Gerda Stevenson
September, 2023

1

a face

the face on the page is
that person i was when
breezes were light, and
every hour without end –

now it watches my gaze,
as i measure how buds
unclench tensed fingers
into parachute flowings

up through ripening air,
there being always that
avid impetus to magnify
what yet holds constant;

between the lines, i will
into living a rosy bloom,
which then remits fresh
seeds to be new growth

across prosaic cheeks,
where there still are, in
what that paper mirror
says, the proofs of life

missing

do you miss your mum,
asks my young daughter,
and i, grandfather old, reflect
how you learn to accept,
let go, move away, yet
there's still a place in the memory
for moments, the smile, the frown,
the face that told so much in silences

and your dad, she asks, my dad who died
when i was younger than she is now, who asks
again, *do you miss your mum and your dad,*
my mariner dad so often an absence;
i remember arrivals, the gifts and hugs,
but don't recall the grading of priorities i allowed,
whether the clutch of comics was taken or
affection's tarry clasp was let, and then to learn
the postcard messages could not be sent,
wouldn't arrive, the absence being different,

the absence being different, and mum,
in her widowed world where kin was close and
cognisant, where i would feel no lack of sustenance,
where her meek laughter was strapped down tightly
by a darkly warding book thick with orders that drove
and hedged her way – such things are remembered,

but do i miss them, could my bones
run artless back in time, to be enveloped
in those blankets of affection and control,
or do i choose to tread my own dark road,
uncertain how it ends, but glad she's there,
my lovely questioner, alive

crofter, not

grow up on a croft,
on an island
with the perpetual
need to be attentive
to weathers
engaged in chores
you might wish
able to perform
themselves

steering cattle to
their grazings
clearing pungent
blends of straw and
dung from shallow
drains under
swishing tails –

schoolwork seemed
starry as our stream
in spate
words permitting live
thoughts to swim
into song
and the smiles
across jotters
you imagined to
be something more –

but then remember
him, stern presence
there behind his
pedagogic desk,

demanding psalms
from memory – hard
labour in the brain,
and all those sums
to do, before sleep
and dreams can bring
release
into a naked garden
where fresh berries,
darkly sweet,
wait to be picked

dobhran

she was shetland blended with spaniel and god
knows what else, first furred sib to my childhood,
remembered as a sleeping coil at the hearth,
a happiness of soot, smooth chocolate and gentle
licks, her only sin to be a rabbiter who'd disappear
for solid silent hours, and once for two dead days,
indifferent to call or whistle, shout or wheedle,
who'd, in her own good time, return, mud-frosted
paws and back and brow, her tangled eloquent
tail entreating us not to be cross. she seemed to
be entirely of the earth

on another day the anguished cackle of hens
might bring my father out, shotgun in hand,
the dog safe indoors for all she barks, his prey's
biast dubh 'black beast' the low hen-killer that
sleeks its hunger out of water and is absent by
the time he's there to take cool aim

at school we read it 'feeds on fish, small mammals,
water-birds', is *otter* –
                            later i'd learn that our dog
shared her name with that invisible enemy,
how *dobhran* was the smart but innocent label for
an out there, blameable, *biast dubh*,

having learned that school viewed my language
as a *biast* too, if not so much black as brindled now

forbidden fruit

1

the biggest nut and
    sweetest to the eye
is on the lowest branch
that reaches out
    above the mossy waterfall

you see it clearly
    from the bridge
and try to count each
    handhold down, with
one eye on the schoolhouse
lest the granite eye be
    watching you

we'll climb down after
    school, you say

2

how sweet that nut was
    just about to be, when
from the bridge, a black-
browed roar sprayed out and
    fell like barbed-wire net
about our startled heads,
        and how
our fingers tingled with
the leathered pain we knew
    would follow in the morning,
but even worse, to see
    the nut we'd

had to throw away
                sink down into
that deep pool, below
                    the mossy
                            waterfall

a voice of authority

fill in the form it says
and i remember how
your breasts plumped flat
as you lay on your back
in the sun's bleached heat,
your forbidden feast

sign on it says
and i remember how
salmon curved its light
up through the spray,
with its urge to nest,
how it stays in the eye,
carved silver spring
against the fall

the dotted line it says
and my childhood, chasing the ball
down that field we wished was level,
the hay we trampled,
our sphere of disobedience

and the nights, always filled
with dark solidities of sound,
uncertainties given bulk,
given eyes, given teeth,
by the quick panic art
of the inmost ear

and the voice says
your contract, my friend

meeting granny

my nose being level
with the soft white edge
i saw her white hair on
the pillow (white as were
the sheets in that white room
her face as white as what
i'd later know was death

she may have spoken,
held my hand, reached
out to stroke my head, perhaps
she handed me a coin, i can't
recall, but that white day could
not have been as sunlit or
serene as it has since become

reel to rattling reel

it came in a van
and was set up
in our wee school dining room

the projector, aimed
at a whiteish screen
on its shoogly stand
was made ready to purr
then reel to rattling reel
the story was spun
for our knock-kneed rows of
breaths held in on backless benches
bright trustful eyes alert to follow
where heroic figures rode, marched, crawled
in their perpetual wars
against cold jackboots, frowning redcoats
or bright feathered heads that always rose
in minatory ranks along horizons
bearing bows and arrows
met by six-guns spinning out
their raucous messengers of death

there was some lore about the 45
among the boys, feeding a jacobite ardour
against hanoverian, imagined broadsword
our chosen claymore shaped from air
ready for the kill

we performed our acts of valour
in the playground during dinner-break
before the hand-held bell and
mr headmaster called us back to sit
on wooden benches hard as brick –

gnarled presbyterian wood
on which once a month we'd sit
watching all those flickering dissonances
where death was possible without blood or
excess demonstrations of agony and grief

it wasn't always john wayne –
jack hawkins (who won the war
five times on land and sea) spread his
stolid english frame across the screen
and the others, under wide-brimmed hat
or metal helmet, filled our sorbent minds
with strutting dreams
of butte or canyon trench or rampart
living through each moment as we rode
or, being soldiers, waded
through sucking belgian mud until
the final reel released us into usual rain

on torchlit journeys home we
held those galloping reins, charged down
our yelling slopes, prepared to board
a veering ship, drove tanks on roads that led
we knew to all that stale old wallpaper
we might pretend was camouflage
when homework could not
be postponed, bed beckoning

and the schoolmaster speaks

now tell me,
exactly,
what is
a poem,
as you view
the instrument of castigation
on his desk

dead plastic crow

what i thought was
the rotting corpse of a crow
in the high bare branches

on looking again, i saw
was the tattered remains
of an old black bin-bag

-----

i tell the class what i've
seen, and someone
says but you're a writer,
so i tell the class it's
just what i saw, what
i thought i saw, and
                    how i saw it

-----

and later, leaving the
building, i see the tattered
remains of an old black
bin-bag, in the high bare
branches, are the rotting
corpse of a crow, with
                    plastic feathers

doors

into
the damp room
into
the dark room
into
the cold room
into
the hollow room
the fractious room
into
the room where one picture frame remained on the wall
into
the variable dictionary of rooms
where definitions redefined themselves as contradictions
the room that insisted on being a room
the room that lacked echo
the room that lived with being empty
the room that was

that one should be
        lined in gold
one roofless
one blood-red and crying
one surrounded by oyster beds
and one, wrapped in lichens, whispers
        its own nightmare
and there's one where the wind, catching
sills and hinges, makes
from their disrepair a rich magnetic song
you'd rather not hear
you'd rather not hear

gaudy jane

o gaudy jane, you are my window on the night,
through you i've watched chiaroscuro turning bright,
the dullest day has blossomed into wild excursions
through deep neon forests where kaleidoscopic fruits
become a warm fermenting sea of joy,
but should i be alone, i know you'll people me
with dancing voices, laughing feet,
the world is baring shoulders,
tonight you are a head of liquid corn,
and words are prodigal,
a dizzy lattice-work of sound

o gaudy jane, you are the glass that parts my lips
in thirsty speech, you lend me eloquence, your lifelong
consonantal drumbeat's dark repeating
abseils from the bated walls,
and should you lead me to the pinnacle
because i have no head for heights, i'll still
be anchored in my reef of straw below –
sipping your golden fire,
the blind headlong warmth of it

o gaudy jane, you are my door into the meadows
of grandiloquent suns, where words not often spoken
flow on seed-rich trades – i'm drunk with you
who dance your long mad dance in this,
my whisky dream, and all the time i'm here
your spilling fingers play wild flutes on me,
and in those liquid falls of light, you radiate
each single match to flame, ember, candle, the spark
that sets all breath alight – the silken gold you wear
has woven rainbows in it, see,
your crystal lips are fire

o gaudy jane, you only ever come to me
at this late hour, and always in the crowded rooms
where secret words are butterflies, your eyes
are glowing mice, luminous shoals, darting this way, that,
shouts of colour all the cautious cry for,
ebonies and purples, crimsons, hinted, random,
spilling – drops and stains of paint – yet still
the deepest and the true, those candid affirmations,
pure bright orange spears of light,
are little gods of mischief and delight

o gaudy jane, you were the flesh of all the janes,
but as you strip each veil away, it's i
who have to face the nakedness of self
i see your breast become a ball of chequered tweed
from which my lips can draw out neither milk nor gall,
just marsh and weed
you are the dogs that smile, as they leap into my glass,
why do you always turn on me –
not happy till you burn my skin

o gaudy jane, it's when that fading joseph coat of fog comes down,
and the hands that beckoned me are wrapped in gloves
the colour of all cavern night – then my sober fears
remove me to those faint remembered dawns
when light was raw and speech was hibernant,
remove me from the heart of things,
and you, my gaudy love,
are still again
and i am the ghost among the crowd

a serious matter

my little beauty
says the bull
stroking
her side
with a gentle fin

          the right whale
making love

all eighty tons of
        tenderness

from a shoreline in skye
for gozo yoshimasu

standing where sea-honed stone
and marram meet, indeterminate,
between the breathing, breathing shore
and nudging birch wood flaked
with sun and drenched in small bird song,
i watch, through cracked binoculars,
a silent heron winging low across the still
clear sea and, with its own reflection, make
a pair of clapping hands applaud its own existence
in toward the same black rock it always
perches on, where crabs the size of toenails
scratch around those pencil feet;

out behind this sentry bird,
a mothering salmon, waiting for a spate,
watchful for seals' appetites, may rise to kiss
the level surface for a quick replenishing fly,
and over on the other shore, a doe
dips light, uncertain feet among dry shingle,
parted from her sisters, open here to hostile acts –
there could still be wolves – her head turns
this way, that – the herd of cattle she's tripped through,
too busy reading meadow's metaphors,
ignores her as she finds an entrance
to the deep enclosing wood;

in this numerous family of slender wands
i hear crissing leaves cross-whisper
beithe, beithe, as if the name itself were
healing charm,

                    and over all,
the smiling mountain,
being a poet of shadows,
makes itself new, always new
(so old, it knows all the tricks)

and at night, the owl, and the shadow

    of a white hotel

at the kelvingrove museum

the young pair in the tearoom
speak
a language without words
his waistcoat says *i*
love you to her hat
they
touch in glances, smile
a kiss across the cooling cups,
but see
his rucksack and her carpetbag
so shameless close as if
in textile coitus
ardent and unblushing
motionless and unobserved
until the accidental
movement of a foot
moves one and
makes a space   stone
eggs or wings in
amber cannot fill,
and ancient engines
never will unite

the shape they make
is broken like
the two halves of
a fractured beaker
locked
in crusts of clay;
and still the eyes
insinuate their messages
(hot innocence)

across that closing
bridge of air

the watcher
is an archaeologist
of love

dusk scene from a high window, glasgow

a clock
beneath its old red sandstone hat
goes nowhere   spins
the usual yarn so slowly
shaggy dogged   it
takes all day

the sun   caught out by timetables
turns blushing red   reclines
its head   bows out

a file of trees along the distant ridge
plays schoolboys being buffalo
dusk-grey and paling into dark

upturned this city wears
a hodden kilt of clouds

beyond an empty church
those tower blocks are filing cabinets
stacked families on concrete shelves

and down beside the unseen river
where indecisive suicides
reflect on whether anger may
be worth the breath   a cormorant
becomes a living spire   salutes
the night   folds into   sleep

while bright whores, dossers,
sleep-all-days and disco-dancers
strobe paving stones and alley walls;
their klaxon wishes, dreams and furies

pursue the moist and shining
constellations of peace or coin or carrion
toward another weary dawn
and   o   like a swift invisible fog
through all the conduits
those sweet hot fragrances
of bakers' vans

edwin

morgan
more can
can more?
canmore
ceann mór
'great head'
aye brims
with poem –
king bard

a journey on words, glasgow to edinburgh

reading calvino on the train while
in the corner of my
eye a young woman
blonde willow
watches me out of
the corner of her eye
while reading
the herald property pages

my book lies open at
the adventure of a reader
that solitary logophile
reading *crime and*
punishment on an open
ledge beside an ocean
while from the corner of his
eye a woman bathing
in the letter-burning sunshine
beckons his attention
out from the almost
pristine safety of the page
his anguish how
to marry touch and
text

across the aisle
cropped gold she
searches for a
place to rest her
head, sinks down
to lay one cheek
against
the letters page

we travel through the dark
both real, not fiction
nothing said
the reader and the sleeper
occupying parallel
not ever
touching worlds

finisterre

littoral of pale gold miles, roused
by wind and smoored by rain,
of rocks as dark as doubt
and storm-punch-drunk,
shades of broken farms
and tangled harbours,
gorse where cattle fed,
hydrangeas in starburst blues
and roses flushed with all the weight
of being rose, sweet perfumes
spinning on the air,
and where once ruins were,
so many empty pristine rooms,
and shrill receding limousines,
the slap of tide against a sleeping hull

it's not all to the sea, this land
of slow green-skirted rivers
praised by bees, of fishing rods,
of knuckled apple trees, clearing skies,
tractors, fragrant hotplates,
clouds of hay and canvas dreams

this season, we toss in
our transient pennies,
primed to buy our portion
of bright traders' wares;
not knowing how to spend, we stand
and hear, among the midnight clouds,
a language, wrapped in faded linen
sing old songs of need and earth
and love and death
and pointed flame

keranterec dusk

the cricket files its song right down
to where, to where the cricket
files its song right down
to where the cricket files
its song right down

the cricket files its
song right down
repeat repeat
until in dusk
a silence fills
that dark atelier

the cricket files
its song right down

the cricket files
its song right down
to where, to where
the cricket files
its song
right down

and all the words
you want to hear
at this late hour
say rest
now rest
in this deep song
the cricket files
its song
right
down

an autumn shift

that leaf is
not a bird
but flits along
the dry path –

colours live
in its weightless
flight
       as if it were
the sparrow it
declines to imitate
insisting it is
happy to exist
as fading leaf

earth will take
good aliment
from its decay

until spring swells
bud into leaf

again

when bill dunn swam the corrievreckan

the day bill dunn swam the corrievreckan
no towrope hidden raft or cork-lined jacket
pumping his unpegged stump against the good leg
staking his life and knowledge of tidal forces
against that boiling cauldron's reputation
against a wedge of reckless wagers
smiling against the frothy residues
that freckled the flat calm kyle

bill dunn calmly swam the corrievreckan
knowing he was no pawn of god or devil
knowing he wouldn't be cut by liquid razors
knowing he wouldn't be swallowed alive by the monster
swimming toward the furious swirl of waters
he knew that pacing his strokes he'd meet the roaring giant
lost in slack, quiescent, fitful as if beaten
between the wild convergent races of ebb and flow

when bill dunn swam the corrievreckan
he passed through the sleep of the chequered kettle
his knowledge swam a sleeping serpent
and shakespeare's brutus might have wondered
whether if he'd swum the tiber
on the cusp between the currents, then
defied his emperor to broach the ebb-tide
or the undertwining flow, it might have given
history another strand to beach on

when bill dunn swam the corrievreckan
lovers cheated, manifesto promises were broken
new paths trodden, rags discarded
nothing was the same again and
everything the same

and today, as a gull
loops in its shifting sphere
of soar and swoop
scavenging for significances, i see
far below the moving
white crumbs of corrievreckan,
a ghost, a shadow, a transparency
upon the water, cut and sweep of
two strong arms and that king leg
kicking against the
humdrum inevitability of death

bandstand

the empty bandstand echoes
with the trumpet-calls of memory,
inviting us to populate its negatives
with all the sounds that overflowed
from when it breathed the melodies
we sense in those old photographs:
ranks of air-filled cheeks, that winking eye,
a stern conductor striving to keep order

now birdsong flits around its rusty frame.
no sparrow says i wish i were
a flautist, happy to explore such silent
shadows on electric wings, as if
to bring it into resonant congruity
with all the absent ears that once might
ask that sharing stranger, neighbour,
lover, to join with them in the dance

an elephant on calgary shore

an elephant nodding its fluid bulk across the sand at calgary
you'd have expected a seal, a basking shark, a school of whales
enacting their drama-for-real, their leviathan lemmings' return;
if you've eaten too well to do good you might dream into being
a gross mutant rabbit sprung out of the warren that freckles the machair
to lope through the tidal –
you might, but an elephant no
not an elephant, a ship gone aground might have rocked in this way
on its keel on the sand, if the tide had come up to its bilges
but the ships have gone, the people are gone,
no circus would advertise here

the butterfly effect

did you ever fart in the sahara
(loud and long)
then look around to
                see if anyone...

more cause to worry that
your cough should swell
a gust
into the hottest swirl
                of blinding sand

but here
on this damp beach
not even the sun exploding
could stir a grain
and you can hear
(from somewhere out to
windward of your present stance)
a foot slap where
the tide is thinking
                to return

a thought

a thought
came bouncing down the hall
as if it were
as if it were

clockwatching

you watch the clock
each second
taking twice as long

what's new, you say,
and, things to do
will take your mind –

is it the case, since
time began, that
this is true,
if space is left

for thinking on, you
must bring thoughts
that breathe life in

so that the crawling
hand can make a
hidden leap around
its face, to bring it

to the mark you need,
when you can see
your love arrive

love in the moonlight

in the moonlight,
no matter how warm,
you may bear death's pallor,
it's the best moon can offer

but having shared your sun-
wrapped noons, bright mornings
and the way your evenings
dance into a fiery dusk,

i know your radiance will
light the darkest road, will
not be smoored by any
pale reflection of this day

on that walk

a plane roars
above clouds

a crow flies –
pulse of wingbeats

they are not related

nor, as i pass,
the thought that
wills, in flight,
my love to you

american sequence

i. first day in america

arlington is
all those clabboard houses
(spell it clap-board) in
the voice of robert creeley
illumination and you're only
four hours down on
yankee soil

then on massachusetts avenue
(creeley's home straight)
a shopfront sign saying

'*long* funeral service'

passing the
boundary liquor store
a glimpsed clerk takes no lip
from hungry drunks
through armoured glass

harvard beyond and
grolier's poetry bookshop
with the floors that sing

and the panelled club
where professor dunn takes
guests for lunch,
oak redolent of roosevelts
and sailing ships
those years
of rich tobacco smoke become
sweet acrid pitch

old boston says
still prim still firm
outside her church
i am no widow

ii. in arlington, between concord and revere

knowing that under
its thin late-winter shift of snow
the park is breathing
i listen

no wind to stretch the trees
frozen in grey from
bole to twig   i have
never seen such grey

birds pause or sleep
jackrabbit does not move
old skunk is elsewhere
sheltering

while silent voices
borne on syntaxes too spare
to shape a language   say
we are still here
we are still

one day into this continent,
an ocean's breadth from home
and i am touched by voices?

their soundless chorus layering
the silent air
even clouds are somnolent –
the pond an uncommunicative mask

not buckskin threats
no wampum plea
to be left alone   only
here   still here
we are still here
not heard by ear but
in the fingertips the ribs

i don't believe in ghosts
i know i'll not see living ice
play sinuous taunting games
to hound me out of here
no vapour takes the forms
of those whose need to
tell a history   lives on
beyond their stifled breaths

we are still here
                    where first
before those pilgrims came
a people walked new paths
and tracked nutritious gods
and tilled where loam was
soft between tall trees

now all i see is this sparse
grey avenue
and frets of clapboard streets
beyond the snow

iii. manhattan i see

here for the poetry gathering, i
                    step into a bright organic
poem
          stone glass steel   the stridency
                    of fire trucks ambulances buses
                         caught in jams at traffic lights and
underfoot   the metal cackle of
                                        long subway trains

this city's a forest   its foliage
                                   stone or glass
                                        reflections, echoes
on the ground
                    perpetual sweat, sibilant shiverings, sinuous songs
spread among the reverberant roots

those buildings are trees
                    reaching for the air
                         and light
                              that trees require

and rumoured crowds underground
who never surface   who are not
shadows   whose limbs cannot be
numbered   who walk among you but
are never noticed
                    whose presence asks
                              if you too
have stepped out of the visible   to be eaten
                    by this city's ineffable hungers

and as you walk the breathing grid, your
          tartan, marmalade, your josephcoat are
                              turned to blooms

all the colours are there
     of leaf and stone, of air and bone
and there are voices
               voices

and in this plethoral city   many singularities –
                   today
a small figure striding, dapper, proud   white mane
like an upstate waterfall   a face
             that says 'was
               always here'

a fifty-year-old squat boy-sailor, wants
      to talk, at midnight, looking for a wharf
     (he's uptown, miles from where the shipping
               used to be)

and always, within the small whirlpool that gives
us temporary shelter   the woman who walks dogs,
flower in her hat, an innocence in straw
beneath the early summer sun

pause   become visible
           and they are with you –
don't ask how they eat
        or what

sometimes it breaks up into islands
      and the street you're on
       is its own   innumerable city
but step down   take that straight
     symphonic line to brooklyn bridge
    beyond the moneyed walls you're near the toe
to which those
     huddled masses were invited

there are still voices   in the shadows and
in the silent mirrors   out among the crouching
roots   and growing
there are voices
                    'we are busy making languages'

and being here   if i
    i cry out loud enough   i might be
heard
            be heard
                    faint cadence on
                            the budding street

iv. coyote plays with custer's ghost

when general custer invited me to lead that charge,
i had good reason then to be elsewhere
besides, it was his and his alone –
that golden glorious dream
i had no wish to be a part of

fingering the wampum belt deep in my overcoat pocket,
i hear the indeterminable song to which the slowly shuffling
circle danced – then, still choking at the rasping coils of smoke,
that pipe was my first meeting with tobacco, shared in peace –
where i had come from that was not the way we sorted our affairs,
each man not a child, an equal voice, i've had my spats with them,
tough guys when they have to be, in kill or coup, they're straight, though,
do mean what they say and speaking pictures, how coyote
dark and grinning padded through our conversations, trickster
who is every fickle kink in arrow's flight path, coyote is the floating bridge
across unbridged ravines the road that disappears in moonlight,
echo of the dancing laugh that cuts through dreams,

and there were songs to keep the necessary rascal busy,
while we painted in the lush lands of our genealogies
those limber warriors who listen as they sleep
whose spilling blood is woven into every child's inheritance,
the mothers, i have watched them stitch a narrative in bead
on seasoned hide, i've seen the way they'd strip a big bull bison down,
the horns, hooves, eyes, ears, tail, gut, blood and every bone
will feed and cut and sew and live

i've learned that pecan groves hit cloud where seeds were scattered
after good campfire, good birth, good death, an enemy attack
fought off with ease, it might have been ten thousand years ago,
to go back's good, pitch camp where earth can recognise
a shoulder blade, a rib a hip, a well-turned anecdote,
familiar lodgepole, traveller come home…

the cones of skin they sleep in have sheltered me from winds
like tomahawks…

we have broken meat together (i wouldn't trade salt mackerel for
                                                          pemmican
or kale for all the prairie's crop of sweet potato)
compared weather lores, we've counted moons,
big straw-bright harvest moons, dark fractured winter moons,
we've climbed between those talking moons
where memory walked knuckles, elbows, back to savouries,
sweet sweats, good skirmishes, a flood, a fever, thunderstorms
the sound of gunfire, rock which smelt of fire,
we have watched a weary flame fold in upon itself, and spark
as one recalled the story of the first eyes on the plain to spot a horse,
another dreamed white shadows, banshee frantic,
building stockades on a broken shore, while shells
like grubby snow creep up their sulking vessel's strakes,
the dreamer told no more,
coyote withdrew from the human path

coyote slept, coyote was a prisoner,
bad medicine was paper treaties –
the dreamer told no more

i could have stayed, become,
i couldn't bring myself to love a blade of grass,
a gnat, a stone, too much of what i had received
of church and school and barrack square still clung,
nor could i live with what my kind had done, but

coyote woke

and danced a ring of agonies and laughter, then
laid down in the valley of the greasy grass to wait
for crimson rain to fall on blue cloth, brass
and heartbeat in the storm at little bighorn

v. eastward at 35,000 feet

but then
a long line appears   that breaks
the night into a rising dawn

up here
among the fitful sleepers
in this tightened air
                    that line, alone

four haiku

1
farmer spreads slurry
over bare fields, stink blankets
air, thrushes still sing

2
a bruise in the field
the red wrecked car, a single
yellow daffodil

3
a tar spreader turns
the old road black again
beside the snowdrop bank

4
like white linen maps
the snow-capped peaks slide under
this long journey south

ravenscraig

remembering still
the blue cathedral
metal naves –
profane silence now
where its furnaces
spat molten hymns
to industry

out among the grasses
tall as gravestones
flat winds saunter
nowhere in particular
whistling thin tunes
through spring

douglas west

at dusk and dawn
the roofs were blue
and sending ropes
toward the sky

this collier street
burned coal on coal,
tied earth to cloud
in plaited cords
of ghostly smoke

the words that make
a family
arose
becoming air

now walls are   air
and gardens
            wilderness

spiders' autumn

wind holds its breath,
the hills are shawled
in goat-hair grey, trees
heavy with weather
cling to their coats;

beyond a fence, manes
shimmer adumbration,
dog capers, chases
sticks, or squirrels (far
too fast for her), and lolls
her happy tongue

on the verges of this autumn
amble, hidden regiments
of hunting spiders have laid
their gossamer nets in tangles
of damp grass; the heedful
walker tiptoes through
those airy fishing grounds,
is glad of bulk,
thanks nature for these gifts

surroundings

open door

sea
    gull beyond

/ white shadow

          gliding

2

decades

prologue

not much to
report, and
everything   that
red battle
to be
      born

1

such relish,
haymaking
that lasts for
          ever
in the burning
sun

2

having seen beyond
the ridge
      to know
the colour of grass
the colour of grass, still
          sweeter there

3

comfortable
in built-up areas
where hunger's roads
glow amber

4

confidence to drive
the thought toward
the brightest furrow
    roadside fields are
    full of blossom

5

wheel half-turned, and
halfway back or halfway there
half-empty or half-taken

6

seconds to the mile
and all seems
madness, gadarene

7

the limit
beyond which all
the fields of possibility
are open,
opens

this land is your land

a picaresque pibroch

my country is a state of mind
where placenames lie like blankets
of distinctive tint and syntax
some half-eaten seams of coal and peat
and fractured syllables congealed
between imported loams brought in
on hard imperial marching boots
where native gods are scattered to the deeps;
faint broken echoes thread unseen
among the underfoot where scribes
and pharisees wear monkish cowls,
speak native tongues and serve
their unseen masters well

my country is a place of peaks,
dark glens where wolves,
intrusive kings and jarls
still shadow-track
the dancing corpuscles of the mind

and yet a land of growth,
of blaeberries and hazelwoods
and childhoods climbing manageable screes
to reach the blood-red glow of rowan fruit:

a boy makes the sleekest ship from a willow twig,
lovers stroll along the edge of tides,
mothers, fathers who have worn their driven days
like bridles, watch their sons and daughters
fill out, grow tall, set sail for always
other places, carrying the dream
inscribed *return,*

to shipyard cranes, and warrens of habitation
storm-battered rabbits would pass by;

and here there are scholars who
trusting one book alone
consign all art and ingenuity
to black irrelevance,
whose nostrums bridle
every one who'd fly or
winged in history remain,
while other musics sweep
the lame, the blind, the dumb of faith
to other spheres of air, and all the rest
must crowd their bright contrary visions
close against the scholars' fractured window-panes
– if glosses of the book are all that's read;
although your libraries were large as towns
the streets you walk are dark forever

here wars are cold flame on a flickering screen
watched by children waiting till the cartoons start
while legislators bicker over articles or adjectives
or punctuation marks and how they will present
defeat as victory or squalid massacre as charity

my country is a web of ways,
each leading to departures from the known,
the stone and timber, warm milk, glowing ember,
words of childhood

here is a dance
where all the young limbs step away
and very few old bones come stumbling
in their limping slow reels, back

my country is a web of ways
of high roads reaching spryly out
and elegiac low roads home,
and there are traces of centurions' cul-de-sacs
and redcoat lines to lance revolts, of drove roads
and whisky trails, sclerotic trunk roads,
scenic routes, slashed hillsides knifed for sport,
of flight paths overhead

my country is a marriage bed
in which raw hopes and bleak
despairs reach out to consummate
unseasonable waspish unions,
where binding oil with water, sand
with air, is easier than coupling
politics with truth –
they have a way, those honeyed
voices, of saying something
other than the shape of what they skim
across the usual seas of ears;

my country is a nest of dreams
where insatiable intruders
pushed the mother's brood
of visions out, and gorge
on all the fattest worms
of thought she brings

and when your land's a rag of shores
where soft boats beach at night
and shadows scatter to the peaks,
a garment torn by winds and tides
its tattered pride still clinging
to a song you hope endures,

this land is our land
there are days when it's dancing,
when primroses and hawthorns shout
o this   is not
the time to live
among the weeds
of feud and faction
this is not the time, o
this is not the time

two crows

two crows
saw through air
in their deliberations
on matters of importance
to themselves

ullapool haiku, mayday 2007

blackbird plays his flute
while rain taps soft nails into
the classroom window

in that fresh puddle
a green tree dances, even
while wind holds its breath

the mountain's white quiff
hangs at a rakish angle,
clouds open their eyes

flags

when you smell the motion of bluebells
when you hear a hoofmark honeycomb
after long summer grasses are scythed –
a fist of angry bees guards their labours –
you know that industry is various, you know
you're not standing in the immediate
vicinity of shining granite flags;
here flags are green, are stalk and leaf,
have heads of gold, pale gold susceptible
to winds, machines and seasons;

while you're not here, you know
the level granite flags you walk
were cut from hillsides such as these –
the gaping hole in great ben X is
all the streets you walk, the bridges,
viaducts, shortcuts, shady underpasses,
tower blocks, flyovers, ocean for shoals
of rushed and isolated humanity
sitting with the radio on, listening
to conversations between
the sharp voices of talk show hosts
and callers speaking down
the tinny line from elsewhere, down
the distant instant meet-the-people,
be-familiar-on-the-airwaves,
never really meeting phone-in line;

you cannot ask the paving stones
to be a mountain again –
the past you've etched in flame
upon your mapping point –
but there's a language here

that sings of grasses, heathers,
brackens, shaped by the distance
or nearness of oceans;

how steep the hillsides
where rocks overhang
where birches grow tall
every field grace-noted by bees
spring is blue underfoot

sùisinis, 1996

i, present here, alone
have human breath
to offer sùisinis
this pale grey afternoon
the wind is silent;
over there the sea's asleep,
the cuillin's great saw masked

but here, where there were
céilidhs, quarrels, courtships, still
the mason's art remains
while hearths are air-conditioned
thatch and thatcher long absorbed
into the turf, the singing wheel
which span at summer doors
is air, is memory;

the stories of old voyages,
from *lochlann* and from gaelic south
which married here, have long since
put on threadbare coats and left,
those tweeds which took their colours
from the rocks and leaves did not
go willingly   their dumb inheritors
(still numerous) have nothing much to say –
a cough, a bleat, a cropped appraisal
of sweet grass, shrugged fleece, while
there an eyeless shepherd's house
still wears its iron hat, red, furrowed, dropping
rust into a skewed and swollen mattress
which sinks through the broken bed as if
a ship of scaffolding gone down were
dragging this dark porous reef, its nemesis

and as i walk among stone vacancies
on these shaven grazings, *any questions*
from my pocket radio discusses how
it's cheaper to feed blood and bone
to herbivores

dead glove

dead glove on lawn
its fingers grasping fallen air
her gardening abandoned
when she heard the
      measured voice that
cut   the music she'd had

                        spilling
through the open window
   karajan's eroica
       while clearing chickweed from
  the poppy beds

      she heard

       radio

    carbomb

      known fatalities

that street   that city   what she did not
know was   when or whether
despite each and every why

and why   so far away
she   could smell ebbing blood

a logical carnivore argues against guilt in jerusalem

cows eat grasses
therefore they are
vegetation transformed

sheep eat grasses
therefore they are
vegetation transformed

goats eat grasses
therefore they are
vegetation transformed

horses also
camels also
here there are
more intricate relationships

all day long
those cows those sheep
eat grasses grasses

transforming vegetation

mutton, beef, must
be defined as
vegetation transformed

in eating mutton
eating beef the diner
only consumes
vegetation transformed

the diner must be vegetarian

creatures of habit

i've done my day's work,
washed, and had my tea
i've seen today's news
                          on tv

then i watch a lion slowly
pad among long grass
                    beside a pool
he knows the antelope will
                    gather soon
around the water's edge
                          to drink

switch channels now, don't
want to see that chase, that
                    raw fanged death
i catch a thriller
                    where the bright
eyed cops speed in pursuit,
                blue lights and sirens
swerve and spin through
                    dizzy streets –
how do i know there's going
                    to be a crash,
the villains caught
              in a ball of flame

why does that comic's catchphrase
make me laugh –

i think i'd like to turn the tv off

i think i'd like to turn the tv off

the flies who follow the lion
know he'll leave
                far more than
those circling
        vultures or hyenas need

and on the late night news
a politician tells us what
        he wasn't asked, again

as lovers fall, like
                moths toward the flame
while blackbirds sing among
                the gravestones

snowhere

watching the fall, it seems at first so
hesitant, but fills, as if a breath spread out
across the land and rested in its composition,
a broad sahara drained of heat and colour,
settled, still, as norm: we listen
to the silence fold us in, and when we wake
the world's put on a bridal shirt and lies quiescent;
nothing moves – no walker's stride observed
                           along the bandaged hill

i had thought the child in me would delight
in sliding down the slope on a dustbin lid
but the eye sees in those obscuring
curves and crystalline blankets
sheer inexhaustible beauty: it's quite
enough to be within, watching:

a wedge of untracked bleached loaves
and sugar clouds, and nothing as it seems
until the trees begin to slowly
shed their veils, chalk sifts…

sun glimpses us, and then another mantle
draws its folds around the seen i sense
the fabric of its hush will lift, in time

we're used to the semblance of sorrow,
banners of tears – this weather has teeth
and hides its boundaries
                           until god's apron
settles on our field and makes
a tranquil bowl – its ceramic brilliance
bewildering the eye

incautious travellers draw in toward
the fiction of a kerb, stop, step out
pause, poise, aim lenses to record as
evidence that curtain of glass spears
imprisoning the neighbour's house

later, walking our northern dog
into that torchlit absence of heel prints,
my daughter says she hates the dark
though even without stars
it could be a cloudy day

                              and morning
opens on a garden hedge besieged by
powder puffs and ears and scalpel teeth,
leaving skeletons of broom, birch, rowan,
thin shadows that will crop the spring

beyond the door, where life
met hunger, pink smirches
on a cold lint skin

had adam not eaten the apple

the thing is
    not to always
        spell the word correctly

let the occasional
        note be flat or sharp

let the flow
        of conversation be   interrupted

a thread of oxide will
        not kill the wine

let the painted cheekbone carry
    a shadow in
    bottle green or mauve

allow the ploughman
        to veer off true
the grain will be nane the waur
        at harvest time

+++++

the choice is this
or
        perpetual joy
a feast of merriment   aye
    with never
        never a pause

can you imagine god
    demanding perfection

for all
 eternity

can you see him
 wake up in the morning
  can you hear him say
 another fucking immaculate day

so reconstruct the bird

so reconstruct the bird
give it the contours of song,
having removed all flesh, all entrails,
bones, feathers, skin even –
synthetics over wire, more
durable, more flexible, will hold
the mechanism to reanimate
this nightingale better,
its resin beak a busy stream
that pours down fluted rivulets of sound
out of the cage
      out of the cage
           where it sits

a bird as real as if
you'd reached out, taken hold of it, and
stroked it gently, endlessly, into its own shape

in the vancouver island rainforest

the big black dog that loped away
across the railway track
was bear
       pure bear
           black bear
the blackest bear
who chose not to engage
with us   but turned
to disappear among
the trees my guide had told me
wouldn't be there   if
the loggers got their way
what they've already cleared
      is visible from space, she said,
as if the far great bear itself
had stretched a starry paw
      and clawed the island's pelt

staying and leaving

when you sailed across the ocean
you did not take the ocean with you,
or the miserable furnishings of your childhood,
only the island, beautiful and priceless, you said,
sufficiency in the cool freshness of its springs,
streams, waterfalls and pools, you said,
as if they
could keep every thirst at bay

that wasn't the song
which filled the tankards
with the tears your ale shed, that
wasn't the hope that kept you
there where the dollars were,
that wasn't the eloquent stream
that kept your throat moist

besides, you won't believe
how rich this familiar water remains –
jewelled spring, peat-brown pool, brine,
brine, time, flight of ravens, and all kinds of
drenching toasts to the health of
those who have gone, and those
who are to come

but, beloved brother, tell me,
are you thirsty, is the island
still as it was in your memory, the sheen of use
on every spade, horse, lantern, the earth fresh,
grassy, the fish-pool still, alive with silver wings,
no thought for withering, for stone or nettle,
does the island (while you're still at sea)
remain as it was (your eye beyond the horizon

where it had folded away), do you
laugh when you remember
how you were, in that cool young time
when you sailed
out through the showers

edited epics

the moon, doing
what she always does:
seeming to do nothing
but reflect

+

the melody you breathe
will sound
across a calendar
that has   no end

+

to watch as tides
wrap round the reef
expecting all the aeons
to have shown a sign
of change

+

when God was born
earth was
centre of the universe
and man obeyed His
silent voice, but
knowledge multiplied
the stars beyond the stars
and turned God loose
to dance alone

+

this pebble
(boulder once)
shines in moonlight

+

descend into the earth
where you extract
black stone
that can be burned
to generate a power
that thickens air

+

you like to wish
you hold
the winning card

+

you ask the clock
to pause –
the air is wine
you want to hold

+

being
the centre of
my own story
gives me choice
that must be read
in darkness

+

each one of us
has looked across a room
to see the one
with whom we'll watch
our children grow

+

that you are
no longer there to plan
the timetable
from which we hoped
to learn

+

each of us can be
that indistinguishable anonymous
passerby

+

clouds having withered, you
may find delight in blue

+

this / poem
was / written
in the / space
between / pauses

a rainbow

always surprises
this one twinned
and as
transient as ever
yet for its momentary life
so real

high up on that pentland slope,
each could tempt
the credulous to plan a pegging
before the golden dig (though
the livestock might not be
quite so happy, nor the farmer,
living with trenches in their
yard) and even if that dream lore
were true, the real gold is
what can be imagined, rather
than those searched for pots –
if found, they could only be
weight in pockets,
or a bright narcotic
spirit in its glass, the radiant
heat that wakes as caustic ash

i'd rather hold this moment
moored on the tides
of memory, hold that tinted arc
as paradigm for what real gold
is worth – rain visited by sun

primula scottica at yesnaby

in memoriam barbara grigor

so small the flicker of a searching
eyelid easily might bruise the life
from it this fragile little flower grows
here where winds are long and
salt and harsh where no botanical
calvin would have chosen earth so
rigorous so sparse to kneel on yet
still it blossoms here above those
fractured cliffs those brutal basting
smiling waters in summer storms
the air it breathes is stiff with brine
this whit of life   still flowers
every tiny purple radiance is lambent
in the blood of time this fragile
little flower grows only here and
on that other ledge across the firth
it could have chosen lusher glens
instead of here the bleakest edge
its season short raw winter long
and sleep exposed to breaking
frost or suffocating snow but then
when all that's left is memory
a film a membrane thin as breath
as small as if reflection of a
distant star fine miracle it blooms
again

translating love
an epithalamium

translate
those bedrock words
i love you into
what they really mean

each pronoun isn't just
its sound or surface, each
is resonant with inference
and nuance

each you and i
is
reef and continent
bland plain and tumult of peaks

each i
carries a cargo of me
each you
is a distant harbour

and though the words
we use may be
identical it doesn't
mean that we are
speaking the same
language

the true democracy of flesh
is shaped by discourse
between heart and head

but heart must trade
and kisses are its coin
while head delivers
aspirations, promises

we have to know
the currency is
tender
      trust
that head will
not leave us
short measure

/

once the ferry love is
boarded, cast off, headed
into open water

there's fun
in ploughing tides
in dancing on
white horses' backs

but we must know
this boat requires that
you and i both
captain, crew, and steer
its course through
stubborn calms and biting storms,
and know
there will be
tropic islands, favourable channels

sail well and wear
the white sails of
knowing
love will carry all
the asks and
ardours
you and i
may bring to this
uncharted voyage
across time's
eternally mutable
ocean
as long as
we steer
hand in hand
hand in hand

we may gather
cargoes as we go

clarity

knowing you have to
    achieve as much
clarity as possible in what you
    have to say to her
you don't want any tears
  to make the rest of it redundant
or the journey that must be taken
    woven into snowdrifts
  before the message has been
 transferred with as much
    delicacy as a violinist might
require to reach the saddest note

some of my best friends

some of my best friends are
some of my best friends

some of my best friends bear
no ill will

some of my best friends
require no introduction

some of my best friends would
never dream of saying *that*

some of my best friends are worshippers
of standing orders

some of my best friends
wear clothes their mothers
chose for them

some of my best friends wear
trusting smiles but
want clear definitions of the *apropos*

some of my best friends
have hair and some have
none immediately visible

some of my best friends
prefer uncertain seas to poetry

some of my best friends have
faith in calendars

some of my best friends drive
dangerously fast or dangerously slow

some of my best friends walk
pianissimo across hot paving stones

some of my best friends
live lives of
sober doubt and drunk contrition

some of my best friends refuse
to crown the power of thought
with trust

some of my best friends carry
unrepentant sacks of indestructible hatreds

some of my best friends are
intelligent women of unspeakable beauty

some of my best friends are
ordinary people

some of my best friends
dislike the moon
its pallor mocks their lust for life
they say

some of my best friends
don't go to school

some of my best friends have
habits
they would rather not have talked about

some of my best friends are
men who recognise
the therapeutic force of tears

some of my best friends wear
psalms like singing waistcoats
even on the hottest summer days

some of my best friends are
jewellers in sound or stone
whose craft is making radiance

some of my best friends have
no desire to cause offence to anyone
but feel they have to say, et cetera

some of my best friends are
big boys who never cry

some of my best friends are
thoughts on the wing

some of my best friends are
women who speak their minds
wearing sensible shoes

some of my best friends are
habitations in lonely places

sometimes my best friends are
thoroughly untrustworthy

some of my best friends have lodging in
those cities far too near the edge
to sleep

some of my best friends are
dogs

some of my best friends are
lighthouses
i define myself by them

some of my best friends are
stones, their shapes make
ancient songs

i want to walk with you my friend
on this side of the road
on that side of the road
i want to walk with you
toward the anvil where
old steel becomes new ploughs

by carlin's loup
for the making new of carlops village hall

from this cold brow,
with its crown of branches,
mystery flies,
as rowan seed,
as light birdsong,
as carrion centuries,
as whispers of sorceries
through the sloping air

have you seen them
in their season
a cavalcade of earthly flowers –
they masquerade as stars

around this stone brow,
frowning with age,
laughter has danced
in hogmanay night
in midsummer light,
in a hymn of reels,
in a stern and holy
cloud of butterflies

have you seen them
in their season
in cavalcades like earthly flowers
they masquerade as stars

on the road where cargoes thunder
hooves alone bore all
the dark and airy narratives
that shaped a history,

built a house of wood
where stories might be told,
in verse or song or dance

let this lichened pentland thumb
throw its morning shadow, where school
and farm and cottage gather among
resonant new timbers, where
we'll recreate the mystery of fellowship
in song, dance, verse,
and breathless pantomime

then you'll see us, in our season,
wearing joy the colour of flowers
make a cavalcade of earthly stars

galina's question

why is there silence, my daughter wants
to know

     i listen, ask her *where* –

outside, she says, and the trees in the garden
seem to have nothing to add, while here the
turned-down radio mutters the morning news

i tell *her it's time to get up, you've school
to go to*, but she wraps the blanket's
warmth around her, *no, it's not dawn
yet*, december's darkness nudges the
window while a truck's growl in the
distance enters the silence –
          *time
to get up*, i urge, while her question
enters my thoughts and grows into a fully
flowering quite unanswerable tree of
never totally motionless   silences

i will each bloom to ripen into an acorn
resonant with space
        in which to shape
           an answer to
              my daughter's question

winter visitors, carluke

seagull in the
low green sunshine
here
on this high frosted ridge
so far
from skerries, trawlings, tides

the sky is clear, the nearest
weather banked away
beyond this ridge of high

another gull comes in
on the cold tail
end of a sickle of air

there's a game to be played
ceremonial dance
and they cut
the shape of a new moon up
from the carpet of grass
into air, pure pale blue air
where the palest curve, as
thin as a pencilled line,
new moon, is
matched by a wing
being caught
in the late sun's glow
they are light
they are light
in the last of the sun
then they turn

into shadow and slide
down an arc of hunger
to crawl for crusts
that schoolkids dropped

as the class, in a heated
room, trawls each
line of words for
sense, sensation, symbol
gull alights
on that patch of green
as gull, as gull, and
grooms a wing, and settles
into the darkening grass

letting my children go

i see my poems dressed for journeys
walk across the unmarked frontiers
at liberty   no need to
    throw a backward glance
i smile and wave goodbye
then turn
    toward this warm yet
unfamiliar place called home

remembering   it's memory
that gives you definition

and that all   you mean to me is
predicate on   *you*   remembered

bed you grew in chair you slouched in
that small variable stretching world
you played and laughed and learned to bleed in

now
how long   before
              slim letters
tell of safe arrivals fresh parameters

and all
the promises to visit me   with rhyme with reason
with the absences the silences   the tricks of
clock of calendar of light

you may fade you may fade
into distance into time
beyond hearing   not
from memory   not from memory
not even if rewritten

and even were i old and cosmopolitan
bring gifts when you return
dried fugu from japan   the echo
from a german train   a peaceful
pockmarked croat sky   a song
as old as skin from ireland   shadow
from the standing stones at carnac
turquoise eye from arizona   please bring
all the strangeness you can find
to mingle with a smell like
new-mown grass   or ink   a page
the always whiteness of fresh milk

between then and now

the hedge between then and now is
a forest shedding its hesitant leaves

the stories you thought you'd never
forget, having scuttered about, retold by
the breeze, on a narrowing darkening
path, are now composting into the cold
cold soil, where they'll feed the worm
that lives and grows and dies among the
listening roots of tall and flowering trees

faith, or hope

the centenarian has just gone out and
bought himself a new suit –
                              why not, he
may have another ten years to go

and there is
                a certain young (almost
pensionable) lady
                    he's got his eye on

so don't be surprised if you see
                                him buy
a buttonhole – a man has to look the part
(though he will be careful bending a knee)

it's not the time

it's not the time
to write a poem about being
a messy eater
        the crumbs i drop when
wandering through the house
with a buttered oatcake in my hand
do not perturb me – sinking
                into the carpet
they can be rescued from drowning
by a hungry hoover
            it's i who am
beyond improving, pondering why
soup droplets defy gravity to find
a track they'll follow down my shirt
why the cup is bound
        to spill around my wrist
and if a curl of lettuce lodges
in my beard it sings *i'm brightly
greenly here*
        but do i let a rose
grow in my cheeks or brow, and
shape a meek return, or else
allow my tousled self a progress
through the broadloom world of
tidal path and honest flaw, where
out of chaos clear thoughts come

the curious eternal

resting his tender head between her thighs
as if to listen for the heartbeat of

                  no longer there

its journey out
          from a dark and private drumming sea
          into the singing air

          how life drew rivers from a nippled hill

how light became
          a jewelled room
          a globe of sky
          embroidered motion of an insect's dancing wing

remembered
          bright eggs fall like rain   into a hatching sea

yet
      such a place
          to be mapping warm beginnings

still, after all those years
the mystery
of flesh, secretions, pulse and breathing patterns

read it again
in the honey cave
braille dancer

touch, but there can be no finding
centre
yet, yet   ever

only those tentative acts of
kindness, love, desire

and the curious   eternal

sky

i look toward the sky, and know
beyond that infinitely clear
                              blue plate
a still   deep   granary of stars
will feed the night its
                    sparks of radiance

endless love poem

but still still
i will write the longest poem about love
i will write it on your eyes
(let them be forgiving)
i will rest it lightly lightly
on your earlobes (feathers)
i will write it on the un-nameable
hills, and the rivers
will come rushing rushing
cool upon your tongue
it will walk with you down
through the seven fields of memory
on down into the still dark glen
where nothing nothing changes
it will swim through every fire
with you (blaze against the tide)
be a star be a radiant lantern
one defiant pitchbright torch against
all the marauding armies rapine
scavenging insatiable as locusts *no*
it will fight   it will fight   it will
not be devoured   i
will fold it in the wrappings of a rose
and loving watch you watch the
fragrant doors curl open (smile)
it will sing out across oceans
blond and lithe with infancy
it will sweep the streets clean into
a wild untameable dance   it
will crash through time
the mechanical forest like flooding
herds of sweet gazelles (unstoppable)
it will run through the pages of every

volume in the unwritten garden
it will refuse to let weary night
claw its ankles eyelids down
it will rise sinuous through leaves
liquid whispers with the sun
were i to call it wine
it would spin
fountain-fresh in the glass
honeyed honeyed still

summer

at a certain time

pink edged clouds
and water

deepening

to purple clouds

and one pale star

a seasonal

as rain draws
moist landscapes
on the window, we are glad
that country they depict
lies out
      beyond

see how, in spite of weathers,
those fields spread out
green blankets

promising

this day is not so cold
that grazing sheep
need to huddle

and even in such
a late month as this,
that field so green
wants to be blue

if morning sun
will blind the eye
that must look east,
there has to be
a way to read
our maps
for hidden tracks
on which we can
believe there is
cold certainty
of home

how a birthplace is remembered

even at distance
and stretching time, our island
stays light in the heart –

we who once lived there
hold its shores in memory,
each stone reflecting

how it's still alive,
although now in distant rooms,
those old photographs

shape three dimensions
with an inner searching eye
where home's roads are loved

last night

last night under a bowl of galaxies
tempered by the white white moon
i knew before this sunset i would see
below me land left behind
and there a rising coast

then in the city with two names
my language would embrace
its sister tongue

the notebook

+

and every time i raise the notebook it
seems as if something weighty might
spread out across a virgin page that,
if words ever come, will soon be maze
of roads to nowhere, swinging tightropes,
cul-de-sacs, or friable cliff edges and, if
i were to be favoured with an opening,
among such tangle, one clear bright
path
    to clarity

+

call the cup knowledge
call the liquor within
        also knowledge
then into the cup stir a grain

watch the grain consume
that liquor, grow, root, sprout
find elbows, crack the cup

find clay

+

only believe, the beating
heart of a poem doesn't
change – it is always new

you observe the day break
like a flower which may be
golden, rosy, deepest blue

which will give you a not
necessarily reliable map
of the weathers to come

if it's rain (again) let the
rivulets' rhythm be neat
let the flow be sweet, of

words that you'll want to
fill out and grow into the
lucent shape of a dawn

such as you'll know, but
have never seen before
an unremarkable grey

bird sheathed on that twig
unfolds to swoop, become
rainbow, dipping into red

+

living in the plastic time
you learn to view
        what's around you
as a synthesis of all
the wrappings which
have bound each day
into a package
        of frustrations
from which

                    there might
be no release

+

no matter
how little
you say
it may
be worth
the saying, if it
touches the edge
of a shadow
that can
(possibly)
be thinned
by a breath
            of words

+

snowflakes in spring sunshine
being
cherry blossom

+

not every
image needs
a word to make
it fit
reality

+

and even after
you have laid out all
your paving sheets

wild nature's roots will
not play ball   a different
game unfurls in
darkness darkness waiting

time will come to
strike for light

+

in full command
of what i need
to know
                    i go

Milton Keynes UK
Ingram Content Group UK Ltd.
UKHW011530101223
434119UK00001B/15